Butcher's Sugar
BRAD RICHARD

SiblingRivalryPress
Alexander, Arkansas
www.siblingrivalrypress.com

Butcher's Sugar

Copyright © 2012 by Brad Richard

Cover Art - Jason Watson

Author Photo - Mitchell Soileau

Cover design by Mona Z. Kraculdy

Sibling Rivalry Press, LLC
13913 Magnolia Glen Drive
Alexander, AR 72002

info@siblingrivalrypress.com

www.siblingrivalrypress.com

ISBN: 978-1-937420-25-3

Library of Congress Control Number: 2012941134

First Sibling Rivalry Press Edition, October 2012

for Tim

There it is.
I gathered the pieces with great difficulty.
(Euripides, *The Bacchae*)

from which autobiography scarcely begins
(D.A. Powell, *Tea*)

Contents

13	Narcissistic
14	Aubade
15	My Sixth Grade Sex Life: Milne Elementary, New Orleans
16	First Love
17	A Changeling
19	The Child and His Monsters
21	Archaic Smile of a Boy
23	Dead Tongues
24	The Men in the Dark
26	Butcher's Sugar
27	Night Lessons: A Writing Assignment
29	Elegy in a Men's Room
30	Eye-Fucking
33	Hermes with the Corpse of Hector
34	My Jesus Poster
35	The Lover Who Would Be Chaste
36	Ganymede: Later
37	Young Soldier Watching Hermes Sleep After Sex
38	The House that Jack Built
39	Self-Portrait
40	My Cat Considers Suicide
41	Self-Portrait as Pentheus
43	Nude Ephebe Reading
44	Sunday Afternoon
46	Mater Dolorosa
47	Self-Portrait as Semele

48   Queer Studies

49   The Cheat

50   My Last Boyess

51   Priapic Murmurs in Middle Age

52   Diorama with Shadow of Narcissus

53   Chimeros

54   St. Roch Chapel, New Orleans

56   The Body, the Word

57   Hermetic Nocturne

58   The Return of Gilgamesh

59   Love Song

60   Hermetic Psalm

61   Poem

62   This Is the Real One

63   Another Poem for the Wind

64   Envoi

66   Notes & Thanks

68   Acknowledgments

70   About the Poet

71   About the Publisher

Butcher's Sugar

Narcissistic

Perfection. Silence.

Dry, autumnal silence. Geese to the north.

His face: slack descent of geese to water.

Water that opened, took in sky, geese, face.

I parted his lips with . . . yes.

Spring, echo of autumn.

"A perfect day." No: a dismantled gesture.

Water without reflection. (His eyes.)

Pool frozen over. Bones at the edge.

No north, south. No body. No here, now.

A day perfected.

Lips parting: ice broken slowly by light.

And then the fluent undulation from above.

Aubade

Naked, I tiptoe to the driveway:
first light shapes
the Japanese plum tree,
the roofs of houses—

all clear, so I run
down to the corner and back
to the shadow of my house,
house of my shadow,

sweating, panting,
my little penis hard,
my body glowing.
My body is mine,

I'm ten years old,
don't know why
these mornings call me out,
afraid I will be seen

or won't be.
I check for hairs,
sniff my armpits.
I have to go back in

before my father wakes up.

My Sixth Grade Sex Life: Milne Elementary, New Orleans

In class, boys passed sketches of tits—mine
drew laughs, a sideways pair of witches' hats.
But I was smart, polite—teachers loved me,

boys didn't trust me, girls thought I was nice.
I had a girlfriend, Suzannah, the D.A.'s daughter,
and on weekends, we made our sanctuary

among trees at a nursery, where we kissed
between lovers' talks about death and sin.
Walking back from church together,

we held hands. Later, on my bedroom floor
with my best friend John, listening to Kiss
and looking at wrestling mags, I wanted

to see John naked, especially his ass.
John was the one who had told me about Scott
getting caught with another kid "doing

a double blowjob"—whatever that was.
Wrestlers flexed and grappled. A double
what? "You know," John smirked, knowing I didn't:

"sixty-nine." Patient pornographer, he detailed
the mechanics of the act. Why would Scott
want to *do* that? (And why hadn't he or John

already shown or told me?) "Sinners die,"
Suzannah would chide, my hand in her blouse.
I hated everyone. My sex life was over.

15

First Love

I'm fourteen, sunbathing on the levee.
Wild sweet-peas bloom in shaggy vines
among reeds at the water's edge. Across the canal,

a man crouches with his binoculars, scoping
the bud-pouch of my briefs and stroking.
Pretending not to see him, to be unseen,

I'm pinned in a moment that hasn't happened
yet for me. Sweat prickles in my crotch.
The canal stinks. Reeds click and hiss in the breeze.

A Changeling

They don't want to play anymore. The muddied field
is cold now when they fall, the grass sharp, stinging,

the ball in someone else's arms. At the game's edge, closer
to the woods (where the sun falls away, forcing out

long shadows from the trees) he sits cross-legged
on his hands, watching the other boys collide, divide,

grapple and tackle, hears their small hoarse cries
before they're smothered by the sky, imagines

the mottled red of berries burst in ice cream
in their cheeks and thighs, thinks of the heat

of a sudden slap, the shamed flush of tears. Tiredness
slows them as he watches, must be what allows a hand

to hang on a buddy's shoulder or sneak down to josh
the easy target of his ass; he guesses their laughter

keeps them in the game. He's not their friend,
their rules confuse his body—so fat, so soft,

so pale, his shame, he wishes himself into woods
whose private terrors he treasures, pushing

past bramble and brush as he hunts
some toy he's lost, almost catches it

shifting away—the Snow Queen's crystal,
a dwarf's ring, a fairy's cloak. Oh, he knows

his game is not for them, but if he could teach them
what rules, what makes him real, more real . . .

He smells winter coming. The last light drains.
Soon, they'll go inside, eat, bathe, knead muscles

whose aches are alien to him. He'll stay past dark
until it's too cold for games, until he loses even this

near-belonging, this green and open playing field
whose outer bounds they concede to him, ignorant

of how, head bent, fingers braiding grass until it breaks,
he imagines those clean, damp bodies, limbs growing

in hidden warmth   *never dreaming how I will grow*
larger as darkness shrinks and chills the field

where we will gather at last as friends
in secret games I rule.

The Child and His Monsters

1.

In the woods, a bird calls the boy's secret name,
leading him out of himself, deeper into shade
his voice can't fill, that swallows it unchanged.

Minnows in a creek shift and dart
as they feed, taunting, knowing his mind
wants to move like this, nimble in its element;
small hand grasping in the water,

smooth stones that feel like skin he knows.
He sees, in currents chill and quick,
his own image squirming out of reach.

The bird eats the worm. The minnow eats the fly.
Monsters eat the boy, all his fear and all his need,
and he grows unknown, apart inside them.
They keep his bones safe where he learns to play.

2.

It's not his monsters he's afraid of: it's the boys
who will not play, boys with other secrets, their games
all noise and blood, casting stones to scatter and kill
birds in a field, boys who yell *fag, fairy, girl.*

In the woods, he watches and learns how to steal
eggs from a nest, how to fish, how to hide when you hunt.
And he learns their speech: *cock, pussy, fuck.*

Still, in their eyes, he sees himself and not himself.
Alone with one of them, he wants to touch
thighs sprawled in his reach; thinks of the pack,
blooded, running him to earth. The monsters watch:

they know a boy's body is not a boy's mind.
They know a man's body is not a man's mind.
They know there are monsters who eat their kind.

3.

The boy is gone: I'm all that's left of him.
Limb by limb in the monsters' belly, I ate the child,
his hands, his heart, and grew into this body and this mind.

Child and game, figure and frame,
form of body shaping mind, mind its body:
I kept my bones safe. This is how I play:

slap and scrape of skateboards down the street,
thrum and whirr of cicadas in elms,
call of thrush and sparrow as they feed,
and then the dragonfly swarm, feeding low

above the meadow in the blood-light of dusk.
Children scatter at the wood's edge, hurl words
like stones. A boy comes looking, listening
for the monster that knows his name.

Archaic Smile of A Boy

Undressing in front of his bedroom mirror—
tee-shirt shucked from torso, socks plucked
from feet, pants peeled down legs to floor—

he pauses, poses a smile for someone
older, other than himself, yet entirely
and always him: a god pictured in a book,

perhaps, limbs loose, at rest from struggling
free from urges of bull or swan, or cries
of boys dying into flowers or stars;

or a charioteer gripping the reins
of his invisible team, hurrying home;
or athlete's body torqued, discus thrown, flown;

or none or all of these . . . He smiles. Outside,
trucks groan, a lawnmower growls, a dog barks
and children squeal. Apart from the day, charmed

by his images, he watches sunlight
from his window change on his skin as clouds
shift and branches sway; touches light and dark

zones of his body; admires the vinework
of veins in his thighs, strong as a stag's;
knows, as fingers sprawl from omphalos

to pelvis, the flux of his mythologies:
a model moping in a magazine,
an actor brooding in his latest role,

a singer whose ballads braid garlands
of cash. He smiles, ignorant, aroused
by the sharp, goatish stink of his armpits,

or maybe cologne he's dabbed on his chest,
a scent without memory, takes hold
of the swollen emblem of all changes

he believes himself master of, and yields,
smiling, to a familiar, solitary chaos,
eternal voyeur, devourer of images,

the one who never smiles back.

Dead Tongues

Kissing a drowsy boy, Hermes remembers
the boys from the agora, who, nightly
after wine and meat and rowdy song,
offered to themselves holy tongues,
each others'. Ah, *langue d'amour*,

speechless, breath and spit and flesh:
what else, thinks the god, did I ever want?
To hell with the past, no more priests
severing from squealing lambs and calves
tongues they hoarded to savor later,

and no more senators sniffing out omens
to trick cities into war and build new temples
on dead boys' bones. Why did they think
I cared what they prayed for? I took
the crisp fat, kissed the boys goodbye.

The boy yawns, smiles. *I love you,*
he says. *I love you, too,* lies the god.
An old ruse. Eyes shut, they kiss again,
but the god recoils, catching an aftertaste
of sacrifice, its ash and grit, its hungry cry.

The Men in the Dark

Dropping shut the trapdoor that opened the dark
above my childhood bed, they don't want me

to tell you about them, those two men
who left their smell with me each night

until I was no longer a boy. In tee shirts
or sometimes shirtless, they sat on bunks

as in a cell, smoking cigarettes and staring
down as I whispered. They liked to hear

about my parents, my dog, hurricanes, the wasp
and the dandelion, how blood tastes, how deaf people talk.

Then, with smoke and a nod, they leaned in to tell me
what made sense only between ourselves: in their world,

there had never been boys, only men. Their mystery
was my world, as strange to them as their bodies

were to me, familiar and never known: they loved
my name, but never spoke theirs. My parents

knew my made-up friends, the ones I chattered to
all day in the yard, playmates I knew weren't real.

These men, though: they had a smell I can't name,
and, if they wanted, could reach down to touch me

but didn't, and disappeared when my hand
reached their doorframe.
                                        One night, they pulled me up

onto the bunk, gave me a stale shirt and a cigarette,
and I slept there and woke understanding their smell,

my smell now, secret stink of the prison
of my body, lonely, alien odor of their bodies

as they dimmed to smoke and voices, like me,
leaning from my cell to tell you, let you smell.

Butcher's Sugar

Beyond the candied peristyle
and sticky portals of the body,

beyond the cavernous boudoir
rank with the carcass of mystery,

in a lowland of swollen cane
chafed by the slutty wind . . .

Whatever it was that sweetened
one's knowledge of the body,

however the epicure discerned
between fit meat and foul,
                                    eat:

too late to say you're hungry
but not for this.

Night Lessons: A Writing Assignment

I took every chance to sneak naked outdoors,
I write, my assignment to be aware of myself

in a defining context, not cruising the park,
you understand, but like when I was a kid,

in the backyard at night, my bare body
no one's to know, hairless, kissed by grass.

So, there I was, and here we are, in the park,
in the poem. The security cop's headlights creep

around the bend of the path, fingering bushes
by the golf course. I know what you're wondering:

Where'd that kid really go at night? Well,
that's hard to say. He lied, said he was in-

side the whole time (dew tickling his thighs).
And whoever this is, shorts down, on his knees

sucking cock every night—you, me,
who cares, he's just a mouth in the dark,

warm, familiar, I write, *but does this* have *to be*
in first person? Bad student, I'm already back

on my bike (it's true, you never do forget),
riding through the park now the sun's down

behind the river, now the joggers and strollers
and well-behaved dogs have gone home,

now it's safe to do this, now I don't remember
how this started again. We should find the kid

and bring him home before something happens
he'd tell. As you know, however, these events

are fictions, like their source, the speaker,
identity a construct, not fixed, broken—I

don't want to do this. Does my not wanting to
make it sexier? *Good question*, I think

at the margin, coasting down the oak-lined path,
slow circle I'll ride from streetlamp to streetlamp,

stopping to take off my shirt, let the damp air
touch me like the lucky ghost of a man

I've met here before, well, more than once, more
than one, to tell the truth, if I have to, even if

I want to take it all back, or else tell you
just enough, you get the idea, just follow me

to that gazebo, who's to know, what's to tell,
moon rising bright as the cop's cold beam.

Elegy in a Men's Room

                              FUCK
FAGS above the toilet paper. BLOW ME
bold in black felt tip. The stalls are empty,
no glory in the glory hole, no suck

but void on void. Foul water, specks of muck,
dried smears of come; air stroked to vacancy
by dingy, anxious light. No mystery,
no key of flesh, no body to unlock:

we swallowed it all. We are what we haunt.

Eye-Fucking

You could say I got a little bit of pleasure out of it.
—Donald Aldrich, murderer of Nicholas West

We drove him way up high out in the park
where it's just red hills and nobody could hear.
Dave, driving, stared up through the windshield,
whistled, and said, *Texas is a funny place at night.*
I looked—just stars and shit, a plane blinking,
the same night I'd seen since I'd been born—
and asked him what the hell he saw
that was so damn funny. Dave, he grunted;
Henry looked over, then stuck his head out his window
and spat. *You are, Aldrich. You're pretty funny.*

Half an hour before, we'd picked him up
out by the rest stop—damn, he was easy!
I stood in a stall and whipped it out,
he went down to it like a kid to a tit
and Dave got him straight upside the head
with one good swing of his daddy's crowbar.
Fucking little faggot. We knew we'd get us one,
and this one looked loaded: gold watch,
chains, big old diamond ring that Henry took
and added to the others on his hand. *Hey Aldrich,*
Dave said, *you think Laura'd like this necklace?*
I told him to get fucked and grabbed the queer's wallet—
bitch didn't have a dollar. I kicked him in the gut,
couple times in the head, then told Dave
to throw him in the bed of the truck,
we'd get paid one way or another.

It's simple, if you think about it: what queers do,
it goes against the natural nature of man. I mean,
animals don't do that. Now, if he'd've had some money,
that might have made a difference, getting back
some of what he'd stole from men like us.
Hell, he wasn't much older than me, what the fuck
was he doing with all that gold? Any man could see
it wasn't fair. So I felt good, like a judge
when we parked and I opened the glove compartment,
found Dave's daddy's gun and put it in my pants.

(Get this straight: that gun was there to *stop* the violence
if he came to and picked a fight.) We dragged him
down into a field, cursing at him all the way,
the gun pressed to his neck. The night air cooled the sweat
on my face; hardly a moon, but my sight was sharp,
catching every glint from Henry's rings, the glow
of headlights passing miles away. *Damn,* said Dave,

dropping the queer, *what's that smell? Skunk?* I sniffed,
then laughed, bent double it was so damn funny. *Aldrich,
what's your problem?* I stood up, caught my breath;
the queer was moaning, trying to raise himself
on his hands and knees. I told them to help him
and yelled at him to strip. Damn, it was funny
seeing how scared he was, not a look in his eye
as he peeled off his shirt, kicked off his shoes.
When his pants came down, Henry turned
and almost heaved, but I laughed so hard again
my sides were aching. I mean, it was hilarious—
when you scare a man so bad he shits himself,
that man is scared.
                    Then he took off a sock
and something fell out: a ten spot, folded up.

I was so pissed, I didn't have to think,
just bitch-slapped him with the butt of the gun
while Dave held him. Henry came up
and shoved him. *Why don't you fight back,*
you little faggot? Ain't you a man? Come on,
hit me! He slugged him so hard
with his fourteen karat fist, Dave nearly fell.
I stood back a second, watching. You could say
I got a little bit of pleasure out of it.
And I planned to get all I could.
The gun came out, easy in my hand,
and I walked up smiling, like he and I
were just two old buddies, took the safety off
and eye-fucked him, passing the barrel
real slow from eye to eye. He was about to pass out,
but don't you know he couldn't help but watch.

I could have done it all night, but Dave said
Go ahead and shoot him, it ain't that hard to do.
So he threw him face down in the dirt
and I emptied the gun into his back, each shot
loud and dry, like when you pop a paper bag.

Some ranger found him, I guess,
then Dave pussied out and they came to me.
Not that it matters much. I'm glad he's dead.
If it happened all over again and I had a choice,
I'd do it all the same. You'll write your story,
and some queer who reads it might think twice
about what he does. And you know what?
Thinking back to that rest stop,
him coming slow from the corner
and that grin he had when I unsnapped my fly,
he saw exactly what he was going to get.
That boy was eye-fucked from the day he was born.

Hermes with the Corpse of Hector

Let's translate together the silence
that makes your skin strange: Troy,
gored syllable, epic of nothing:

after your baby's brains are bashed
and the wailing women have borne away
their sorrow without shore, after the stink

of the burning town, your pyre magnified,
has scared into the hills a few deer
who steal back next spring to browse

in orchards tended by a fitful wind,
this silence breathes, this absence feeding
on you as gods and maggots feed.

Greeks bicker over funeral game trinkets,
I talk to dead men, your father chokes
down gobbets of grief and pride—sick,

I am sick of the wisdom of war:
when his sword kissed your neck,
you learned the heat of a hero's death

makes heroes hard, you felt him fuck
your name into dirt, make you strange
where you lived. And it fucks a hole in me

through which you and your silence pass
along with a few archaic yelps,
oily smoke, timid deer, the wind.

My Jesus Poster

Pinned to the back of my bedroom door
when I was eleven or twelve, he stared,
not, I thought, imploring the father
who forsook him, but mercifully down
on me, the little sinner who adored him.

Never did my image mirror his—
sallow skin taut over muscles stretched,
stomach caving in, the twinned shadows
of his pubic bones bent to meet unseen
beneath his loincloth's twisted folds—

and yet he was my image of man
for me as yet unmade. My grandmother
gave me the poster so I would learn to love
him as she did, as she loved me. *Love ME,
love ME!* I prayed, but his honey-mild gaze

hardened like amber the harder I beseeched him.
"Who's this?" my grandmother hissed
to my father the last time I saw her.
Who knows what she knew then? Not me.
I learned in a Biblical Lit. class

how gravity kills the crucified:
the slow rip of bones from sockets,
ribs closing in, crushing breath from lungs,
the body's weight squeezing out the soul,
whatever that is, I'm twelve, I'm holding tight

to all I know, oh Jesus, let there be more.

The Lover Who Would Be Chaste

You say I lack, but that's a lie:

I have myself and my disregard
for false interiors. Let surface
suffice, grant me the infinite
promise of skin, immaculate
as photographic paper never lit.

There's a system I devised
that fixes the distance for desire
precisely: your shadow comes just
barely to mine, but dare not risk
infecting my pure image with your own.

I know exactly what I need:

I know I'll know it when I see it,
the way a mathematician sees truth
poised weightless on the point of proof.
Love? That's just analogy, marred
by thinking two make more reality.

If you insist, I'll let you touch me
somewhere where it doesn't count, a place
I can seal off and forget. —There;
I did all right, I think. Embrace
my image in you, if you want. I want

to float like light on water's thoughtless flesh.

Ganymede: Later

Pale, spanking-naked, smooth as dolphins,
the new boys play in the pool.

I hate them. Their laughter shatters
across the tiles as I step

among puddles, towels, candy wrappers,
carrying Big Daddy's booze cup

to him sprawled in his chaise.
He takes it, sips, pats my butt

without a glance. Old slob, a pearl
of ambrosia caught in your cloudy beard,

do you know what they know?
The talon's pinch, the lecher's breath

in the eagle's beak. Eyes quick as fish,
they're checking me out. They're thinking

getting flabby, won't be long, he's
no prize for Daddy's lap. Boys,

when you've sneaked your share of sips
along the way, acquired my taste

for god-stuff, you'll learn the lust
that drags your beauty down,

that bloats you as you drown.

Young Soldier Watching Hermes Sleep After Sex

When he fucked me, it made me think
of when I'm inside a girl and I want
to know how it feels to be fucked by me.

The way he sleeps, it's like he knows
I'm watching, like he's dreaming me
just like I would if I were him.

He says he's a god.
Whatever.
I could fuck him too.

The House That Jack Built

Sometimes he thinks he cannot bear the smell
wafting through the heat ducts from the basement,
earthbound odor of boys he sent to hell.

Ghosts cloud his TV screen, and he can't tell
how they got there. Each channel shows him torments
he sometimes thinks he cannot bear. The smell

has seeped into his closet, a charnel swell
fills his shirts and pants. Lysol's no effacement
of the earthbound odor of boys he sent to hell.

It's even in the attic. If I fell
and died now, I'd suffer no abasement,
he sometimes thinks. He cannot bear the smell:

it taints his steak and green beans, makes him ill.
Night's worst, some scents recalling what a face meant.
That earthbound odor of boys he sent to hell

sighs from his pillows, casts its strangled spell
on dreams his waking covers like cement.
Sometimes he can't even bear his own smell,
earthbound odor of boys he sent to hell.

Self-Portrait

The withered branches, the flaccid,
frost-browned leaves of the poinsettia bush;

the sunlight pickled in my whiskey glass
when I slump at my desk at noon;

the sick mirror of my computer screen,
leer of the corpse that greets me there;

the sorrying whine of the wind
shuddering the poinsettia's leaves;

scrape of a blade honed in the heart.

My Cat Considers Suicide

He watches the slow blades of afternoon,
how painlessly they pass through the oak leaves
then hone themselves in the windowpane
and take steady aim at the place past his eyes
where his last glance waits.

The light looks cold, but feels warm
on his fur when I touch him. See,
I want to say, it only looks empty.
I mean the day, the sky . . .

I've lived what I am this long.
The light grows sharper.
My cat's fur shivers, his eyes
narrow shut. Can't touch him.

Sky a bloodless blue.
Each leaf a separate death.
His glance meets mine.

Self-Portrait as Pentheus

Prelude (Foreplay)

Dismem-
ory: the afternoon light

fumbling shadows, your hand
sweating on my thigh

Love, leaf-scatter

I hate the sound of dead things
the wind scrapes down the street

how can I re-member
what I am before you

Love(un)making

What I wanted to say

makes figures depart

the story no one comes home to

dressed in festival furs

the sky swells a wineskin

I alone refuse to drink

chastely or not entirely of the will

of one body by ourselves

I am never other enough

Afterplay

Maybe no future

but my body the sorrow
of a god disembodied

no mother to gather
my shadows together

pooled bright and dark
in a live oak's roots

I am not fresh rain

Nude Ephebe Reading

He sweats a little, turns the dull page
and the afternoon light on the beach
turns with his mind and body. The book,
awkward in his lap, is nowhere

he finds himself, knows nothing he wants
to be. Bored, he shuts his eyes, lets the wind
undo the words so they touch themselves
in him, ephebe, savant, young chaos

of heat and water churning grit, grinding
sky down to glittering bits, particles shattered
into nothing less than self, as a swell

gathers, holds, breaks in syllables of spray
falling, swallowed back into the changes
of what one is, wave and body and text.

Sunday Afternoon

God-sick, boy-sick,
the lover rises from the studied bed
where he has lain alone all afternoon,
considers this morning's tepid coffee
and the clutter of books and magazines,
shakes off a chill, and lights a cigarette.
The rain has stopped, and now a gray-green light
declines to this lover, his smoke and skin,
as he again rehearses in his head
love's colloquies, this lover now unmoved
by strands of sun-shot rain-beads on a branch.

No god, no boy,
in all his smoke and tepid colloquies,
speaks for the lover; nor are they the source
of love and sorrow, all the lexicon
the lover owns to script his dialogues
in which he plays now god, now boy, never
wholly either, himself. He dwindles down,
his words dwindle . . . Fresh coffee and a book
might shift the burden of this monody.
A bead slips from the branch; he feels a loss.
Whose absence is this, so clear in late light?

A god of stone,
or wood, or flesh imagined: that's all,
the lover knows, that's all gods are. And yet
he has dreamed, in stone, in wood, and slick pages
of magazines, and brittle words in books,
god after god more real than he could love.
And he has lain nude in grass after rain,

a boy alone as a god with his world.
He studies the bed, steadies his body,
dizzy as he clings to the flimsy thought
that he is more or less than real, unloved.

"A pungent boy,
orange-fresh, more delightful to my loving mouth
than all my stale and pallid colloquies—
basta!" He snuffs the cigarette, a squirrel
jumps from the branch, shaking free the last beads,
now lost in the gray-green depths of the day.
Time to put away these books, make the bed,
put gods and boys to rest, clear out the smoke
and breathe unthinking air. He lifts the sash:
the whole sky holds a brilliant orange thought,
brightness out of which the night will be born.

The lover loves
his absence, what is himself no longer,
no lover. Here is coffee no one drinks,
the book no one reads all night as he lies
reading alone in his unstudied bed,
pausing now and then as if to respond
to something some god or boy might have said,
words that ripen like oranges in moonlight.
But the moonlight finds the branch clean and bare,
there where the sun was supposed to have made
a gift of the last, frail beauty of the world.

Mater Dolorosa

Sky is sky: I doubt it remembers
the story of the sorrowing mother.

Outside the church of Mater Dolorosa
stands a slightly less than life-size Jesus, safe

among philodendrons, behind an iron fence;
arms lifted, face uptilted, he, too,

seems puzzled by some absence. Vigilant,
he scans the sky: satellite, jet,

shuttle of swallow and pigeon.
The faithful must keep her inside,

where I never go. I admire the doors
when walking past to the drugstore.

Maybe her son isn't even the reason
for her sadness anymore.

No one rings the bells:
gears do the handiwork.

Seven o'clock: another fiction
to remind me I'm still here.

Self-Portrait as Semele

Drunk, I watch the lightning
                              across the lake.

No thunder. Tremor;
                  cloud-dulled flash,

spasm in the nerve-web.
                         A fat moth

maddened by porchlight
                        jerks on its back

right next to me—

                 Your annihilating kiss.

Queer Studies

Everything there is to know is known
by little boys. Vanity, wretchedness,
holy boredom: he reads it in the softness
of slim fingers, smooth thighs, has been blown

to belief by a mouth too full to groan.
A boy is a book to be undressed,
his lover holds the key that will caress
wide open wisdom's inmost door. Alone

is all his studies leave him. Wiping clear
the bathroom mirror, it's not himself he sees
but a troubled scholar with a stubbled jaw,

eyes fixed on a figure that disappears,
erased from the index of memories,
a sky corrected, blank as love or law.

The Cheat

The boy sleeps. I drink. The wind
shuffles its deck of ghosts—
a game to kill some time?
My hands pretend to play,

shuffle the deck of ghosts,
fill my glass with the boy's face.
My hands pretend to play
as if they wrote the rules.

I empty my glass—his face
tells nothing of his dreams.
As if he wrote the rules,
he cheats me like the wind

and lies about his dreams,
little mirrors refusing me,
cheating me, like the wind
dealing out every face

but mine.
I'm saving my move.
I'll palm his face
and hide it in night's hand.

You're safe—don't move.
Killing time's a game.
Hidden in night's hand,
the boy sleeps. I drink the wind.

My Last Boyess

Sing? He sang. Hear it,
shiny fish song
under my cold tongue?

Play? All his pieces
fell away to me,
his love to lose.

He unzips his
silence, I fondle
his nowhere, we suck

a long going dry.
My past is brittle
where I kiss it.

Do? He outdid
undoing, flower-
bound, swallowed the

wasp, the razor.
A moth's shadow
worries my lamp.

Wrong? Nothing
's wrong, all's fit
beheading a void.

What squirms
in my mouth
I swallow.

Priapic Murmurs in Middle Age

Your skeleton
rearranges my nights to no end. Or as if

a map unfolds itself where there had been
no place to speak of, pinned by one corner

to the nursery's window frame, rattling
every time the giant breathes. So long,

all those birthdays in the barn, in the dark
the wind took, the flicker of your skin

all I recollect of light, then this lateness
none belong to, long for. The giant drowses

under my window, among the hydrangeas, rubbing
petal-shadows from his eyes with baby

knuckles, blushing.

Diorama with Shadow of Narcissus

The artist has rendered the Death of Narcissus
as a dark pin-striped young undertaker
seated on a folding chair beside the corpse
at the pool's edge. The artist considered
letting the corpse lie *in situ*, face down
in the water, or propped up as if snared
still in reflection. Instead, the boy kneels,
turned toward Death, not meeting his gaze.

Grief presents itself in various figures:
crepe leaves of generic trees flutter
in the breeze from an oscillating fan
also disturbing the surface of the shallow
unconvincing pool, "water" too clearly "water."
A "songbird" calls from the "woods"
repeatedly. A fluorescent tube's flicker
enacts an anxious crepuscule. Painted
as distance, the sky represents nothing

the boy sought, his "corpse" no more real
than his desire. The viewer shivers, chilled
by shadows unfastening from bodies,
shaking loose from failing light. "Soon,"
states the artist, "Death, being in love
with itself, will also disappear. The pool,
polluted with images, will stagnate.
Your departure will leave my shadow less

than what remains, believing less and less."

Chimeros

A guy at the gym spreads his legs
and when he catches me looking, he's the one
chasing a frisbee across a field, his shorts
slipping down his ass as he runs; he stops
to hitch them up, and he's the produce clerk
whose armpit scent, sharp as cilantro,
makes me linger, afraid if I turn I'll miss
the three boys in line at the movie, the boy
across the aisle on the plane, the boy whose smile
crumples when I smile at him, the boy . . .

O crippled automata of my heart!

St. Roch Chapel, New Orleans

The iron-grating gates stand ajar. It is St. Roch's Cemetery, known
of old as the Campo Santo . . . *[A]fter the awesome yellow fever*
epidemic of 1878, people began to flock to the shrine of the saint who
was especially invoked in cases of affliction, disease and deformities.
(from the guidebook to the St. Roch Chapel and Campo Santo)

The saint lifts the hem of his robe
to show me the wound on his right leg.

In the festering light of five or six candles
and the steady hiss of rain eroding the day,

I've come back alone as if for comfort
to this cemetery's half-forgotten shrine.

I touch the wound, where robbers stabbed him,
then the small dog at his feet, his earthly companion

as he wandered, destitute, healing plague
until he found his way home; his townsmen

took him for a spy, jailed him and let him die.
Patron of this yellow fever parish, he intercedes

for the terminal and invalid; even filmed
with dust, his skin looks youthful, alive:

I would kiss his dark sore if it would give
either of us solace, if it would bring back whole

companions who died from the wrong touch,
whatever killer stole their love. He watches

as I walk to the locked grate of the alcove
where the sick have left their offerings:

a baby's shoes, a baby's back brace,
a corset with stained laces and rusted stays,

plaster casts of organs—heart, lung, liver—
dentures, a plaster hand hung upside down

from a hook in the wall; scattered on the floor,
age-bleached polaroids of smiling loved ones,

grimy stuffed animals, prayers scrawled
on business cards, post-its, scraps—

suffer us, who are nothing, and live
knowing you cannot help but see

yourself in our broken image, a body
imprisoned in terminal hope, God.

The Body, The Word

He tried to make a body out of words,
to make of words a body, he tried

to write himself whole again, a self
wholly written beyond himself, the words

one body, himself as written, but every word
said *no, I am not you, you cannot write*

me in your image, he kept writing, the body
found itself between the words, its image

the unreadable space he wrote in, he lived
between the body and the words, they made

him write, *who do you think we are, we are*
nobody's friends, we speak what we speak

beyond you, but they spoke to no one,
he no longer wrote, the words went on

without him, glad to move as one body
meant as said, while with them unspoken

strange flesh moved and made all unknown.

Hermetic Nocturne

after rain a cloud-filtered light in oak leaves
    dusk's scent the shadow of a man
        and I don't know who I am

machines on the river hammer and thrum
    in every breath a sting a soreness
        and I don't know who I am

scuttle of paper bags stirred by a rat
    day's last glitter in a crack vial
        and I don't know who I am

a mourning dove moans in a Japanese plum
    a fly whines at the windowpane
        and I don't know who I am

patternless sky ransacked of meanings
    cool balm of grass against my feet
        and I don't know who I am

a camellia's bruised petals a reminder
    husk of the moon in a puddle
        and I don't know who I am

a child's face eclipsed by a mother's hand
    rain cupped in the live oak's roots
        and I am not who I am

black passion of ants at a junebug's corpse
    star's last spasm

The Return of Gilgamesh

who are you now at the prison gates
at the cratered road's end a prison

where your palace stood your odor
of marsh and cedar smothered in smoke

from the ravaged library the songs
of foreign soldiers confuse you

as you stumble through sullen crowds
and turn toward your palace again

veiled in mortar smoke and dust the prison
a soldier's howling bride she leashes

the crowds and jerks them inside her
where they lick and cower she touches

your skin coarse as withered petals
of the immortals' weed of life

whose thorn scrapes at your heart
as a stylus a tablet of clay

where the bride the soldier now scrawls
in her carrion tongue the story

of the hero limping home alone
to his palace his prison his bride

Love Song

Brother   splintered cedar   wounded dove
       Sky-fallen ax I embrace
    Cannot lift you when I kiss

     Broken song you teach the air
   To suffer   punish angels
     Explode your heart in prayer

     Your heart   god's rubble
Hollow water   crippled rose

Grave refusing
    Shelter for my bones

Brother who shatters
   Who utters us home

Hermetic Psalm

Say one note, or no note: a spasm,
a pinch of the lyre's string, say

what you need of the god you hear
in the twang of fingertip and wire,

a song unsinging the god, ache
waning in blood and bone and air,

and no kiss, no falling together of word
and body, body and world, no singer

to sing world and you as one note
held whole in the god's ear. Listen:

the god caressing your spine
is this song forgetting you.

Poem

for Reginald Shepherd (1963-2008)

Your voice is all afternoon, your voice palace
yielding to palace-no-longer, sky sounded
to depths I call to, whatever calling back.
Your voice all I want, unheard. No weather
or whether, not this shirtless man or that,
shaping the afternoon he jogs in rain
along my avenue. Death is no god
no longer, nor you, nor I if this song
make new or the world undoes. Unkind,
unlike, death cannot imagine you as I can,
rain falling in empty streets, almost.

This Is the Real One

I think

About Reginald's death so often
Every line is terminal

He never said he wanted
This dearth of images

And who wouldn't rather swim
Naked all summer I wrote

Across the bottomless page
More likely now these erasures

In what he called my song
So I call his answering machine

Just to hear the voice of
Ghosts I don't believe in

If I'm still the one breathing
Is a body worth having

I have in mind

Strauss' *Four Last Songs*
As recorded by Jessye Norman

Playing in a church in Florida
Although I am an atheist

I took communion sincerely
Yours I told myself

(Meaning his) I understand
The music   not the words

Another Poem for the Wind

A stillness in the grass, yet the hickory leaves churn.

Faded ribbons on a maypole twitch, a spirit's rags,

air tearing itself apart, sifting specks to the ground,

anxious to build a boat for the hero's ghost

to row across the meadow, no homecoming,

nothing will come of this, nothing ever comes.

Envoi

Slowly the rain
      thinks :
            jasmine
            thistle
            withered fingers
            of the poinsettia
                budding—

Light empties
      from the sky's face   :   shadows
          heap on shadows, leaves
             fallen from a psalter

The jaws of the hour
      relax

  You beckon

I enter   am broken

    spoken

Notes & Thanks

"Eye-Fucking" is based on the murder of Nicholas West in Tyler, Texas, on November 30, 1993. West was picked up, robbed, assaulted, and killed by Donald Aldrich, Henry Dunn, and David McMillan. Aldrich repeatedly claimed that his actions were justified because West was a homosexual; sadly, however, many of the most outrageously homophobic public statements about the murder were made by Texas legislators and other public officials. McMillan, a minor at the time of the crime, received a life sentence for aggravated robbery and aggravated kidnapping. Dunn was executed by lethal injection on February 6, 2003, and Aldrich on October 12, 2004. In Aldrich's last statement, he apologized to West's family.

"The House that Jack Built" is loosely based on John Wayne Gacy, who brutally raped and murdered at least thirty-three young men in the Chicago area between 1972 and 1978, burying twenty-seven of them in the crawl space of his house. Gacy was executed by lethal injection on May 10, 1994. Although my poem's unnamed protagonist appears haunted by guilt over the horrors he has committed, Gacy remained unrepentant to the end; his last words to his executioner are reported to have been "Kiss my ass."

Books formative in conceiving and writing some of these poems include *The Homeric Hymns*, translated by Apostolos N. Athanassakis; *Hermes, Guide of Souls*, by Karl Kerenyi, translated by Murray Stein; *The Eternal Hermes*, by Antoine Faivre, translated by Joscelyn Godwin; and *Greek Homosexuality*, by K.J. Dover.

"Self-Portrait as Pentheus" is dedicated to Reginald Shepherd (1963-2008), without whose unflagging encouragement much of this book would not have been written.

For their critiques and kindness, I thank and am indebted to: Peter Cooley, Anne Gisleson, Carolyn Hembree, Lois Hirshkowitz, Major Jackson, Kay Murphy, Cin Salach, Paula Sergi, Ed Skoog, Dana Sonnenschein, Elizabeth Thomas, Tom Whalen, and Andy Young.

Finally, I am deeply grateful to the Ragdale Foundation for residencies that were crucial for writing some of these poems; to the Surdna Foundation and the Louisiana Division of the Arts for generous support; and to Paul Willis and the Saints and Sinners Literary Festival, where I was fortunate to meet Bryan Borland, who encouraged me to send him the manuscript of this book.

Acknowledgments

Grateful acknowledgment is given to the editors of the journals and other publications where these poems first appeared, some in slightly different form:

Barrow Street: "Love Song"

Bayou (University of West Florida): "Another Poem for the Wind," "Dead Tongues," "My Cat Considers Suicide," "Priapic Murmurs in Middle Age," "Young Soldier Watching Hermes Sleep after Sex"

Bayou (University of New Orleans): "First Love," "Hermes with the Corpse of Hector," "The Men in the Dark"

Del Sol Review: "Hermetic Psalm"

Hogtown Creek Review: "Mater Dolorosa"

Hunger Mountain Review: "Archaic Smile of A Boy," "The Body, the Word," "Chimeros"

The Laurel Review: "Poem," "Self-Portrait as Pentheus," "Self-Portrait as Semele"

The Ledge: "Ganymede: Later"

Meena: "The Return of Gilgamesh"

Massachusetts Review: "Night Lessons: A Writing Assignment"

New Orleans Review: "St. Roch Chapel, New Orleans" (as "St. Roch Campo Santo, New Orleans")

North American Review: "A Changeling" (as "His Kind")

Phati'tude: "Butcher's Sugar," "Narcissistic," "This Is the Real One"

Western Humanities Review: "The House that Jack Built"

Willow Springs: "Queer Studies"

Witness: "Eye-Fucking"

Several of these poems appeared in the limited edition chapbook *The Men in the Dark* (Lowlands Press, Stuttgart, Germany, 2004).

"My Sixth Grade Sex Life: Milne Elementary, New Orleans," appeared in the anthology *Bend, Don't Shatter* (Soft Skull Press, 2004).

"The Body, the Word" appeared in the chapbook *Curtain Optional* (Press Street Press, New Orleans, 2011).

About the Poet

Brad Richard is chair of the creative writing program at Lusher Charter High School in New Orleans. A native of Texas and Louisiana, he received his B.A. from the University of Iowa and his M.F.A. from Washington University in St. Louis. He has published two other books of poems—*Habitations* (Portals Press, 2000) and *Motion Studies* (The Word Works, 2011—Winner of the 2010 Washington Prize, finalist for the 2011 Thom Gunn Award for Gay Poetry from The Publishing Triangle)—and two chapbooks, *The Men in the Dark* (Lowlands Press, 2004) and *Curtain Optional* (Press Street Press, 2011). Richard is the 2002 poetry winner in the Poets & Writers, Inc., Writers Exchange competition, and his work has appeared in a wide range of journals, including *American Letters & Commentary, Barrow Street, Bayou, ConnotationPress. com, Hunger Mountain, The Iowa Review, Laurel Review, Literary Imagination, The Massachusetts Review, Mississippi Review, New Orleans Review, North American Review, Passages North, Prairie Schooner, Sakura Review, Satellite, Western Humanities Review, Willow Springs,* and *Witness.*

About the Publisher

The mission of Sibling Rivalry Press is to develop, publish, and promote outlaw artistic talent)—those projects which inspire people to read, challenge, and ponder the complexities of life in dark rooms, under blankets by cell-phone illumination, in the backseats of cars, and on spring-day park benches next to people studying Thom Gunn and Harryette Mullen. We welcome manuscripts which push boundaries, sing sweetly, or inspire us to perform karaoke in drag. Not much makes us flinch.

www.siblingrivalrypress.com

CPSIA information can be obtained
at www.ICGtesting.com
Printed in the USA
BVHW071331310319
544161BV00001BA/292/P